To

From

Date

SOMEONE CARES

PHOTOGRAPHY COPYRIGHT © 1996 BY VIRGINIA DIXON

TEXT COPYRIGHT © 1996 BY GARBORG'S HEART 'N HOME, INC.

DESIGN BY MICK THURBER

PUBLISHED BY GARBORG'S HEART 'N HOME, INC.

P.O. BOX 20132, BLOOMINGTON, MN 55420

SCRIPTURE QUOTATIONS MARKED TLB ARE TAKEN FROM THE THE LIVING BIBLE

© 1971. USED BY PERMISSION OF TYNDALE HOUSE PUBLISHERS, INC.,

WHEATON, IL 60189. ALL RIGHTS RESERVED.

SCRIPTURE QUOTATIONS MARKED NIV ARE TAKEN FROM THE HOLY BIBLE, NEW

INTERNATIONAL VERSION® NIV®. COPYRIGHT © 1973, 1978, 1984 BY

INTERNATIONAL BIBLE SOCIETY. ALL RIGHTS RESERVED.

JANET L. WEAVER WISHES TO THANK JOAN M. GARBORG FOR HER EDITORIAL

DIRECTION AND WENDY GREENBERG FOR HER "APPLES OF GOLD."

ISBN 1-881830-28-4

Someone Cares

Photography by Virginia Dixon with featured sentiments by Janet L. Weaver

May God send His love like sunshine in His warm and gentle way, to fill each corner of your heart each moment of today.

The rainbow of God's promises is always above the trials and storms of life.

....

CHARLES SHEPSON

I have buckets of God's sunshine to brighten up your cloudy skies.

I'd like to help you find your smile again.

May you grow to be as beautiful as God
meant you to be when He first thought
of you.

Delight yourself in the surprises of today.

Whenever I think of you, I smile inside.

God makes our lives a medley of joy and tears, hope
and help, love and encouragement.

A gentle word, like summer rain, Can soothe our hearts
and banish pain. What healing comfort often springs
From just the simple little things!

*Gentle touches
sweeten sour
days.*

Joy finds no bounds in its exuberant dance upon the sunlit fields of hope and healing.

*I have loved you with an everlasting love; I have drawn you
with loving-kindness. I will build you up again and…you
will take up your tambourines and go out to dance with
the joyful.*

....

JEREMIAH 31:3,4 NIV

*That I am here is a wonderful mystery to which I will
respond with joy.*

May you be ever present in the garden of His love.

As Jesus stepped into the garden, you were in His prayers. As Jesus looked into heaven, you were in His vision.... His final prayer was about you. His final pain was for you. His final passion was you.

MAX LUCADO

Exalt with me and let us praise God together. In His garden we find such joy...such vibrant displays of His passion for us.

You are tenderly
loved by the One
who created you.

❧

Every single act
of love bears the
imprint of God.

You are...infinitely
dear to the Father,
unspeakably precious
to Him. You are
never, not for one
second, alone.

NORMAN DOWTY

Flowers leave their fragrance on the hand that bestows them.

Those who bring sunshine to the lives of others cannot keep it from themselves.

....

JAMES M. BARRIE

The best gifts are tied with heartstrings.

*Every gift
of kindness
bears the
signature
of love.*

You are God's
created beauty
and the focus
of His
affection and
delight.

Because of what Christ has done we have become gifts to

God that he delights in.

....

EPHESIANS 1:11 TLB

God will never let you be shaken or moved from your place

near His heart.

....

JONI EARECKSON TADA

Friends warm you with their presence, trust you with their secrets, and remember you in their prayers.

How precious it is, Lord, to realize that you are thinking about me constantly! I can't even count how many times a day your thoughts turn towards me.

PSALM 139:17 TLB

*Your whispered
needs become
my constant
prayers.*

I'd like to help you reach your highest dreams and watch you paint new horizons with the colors of your soul.

Hold fast your dreams! Within your heart keep one still,

secret spot where dreams may go and, sheltered so, may

thrive and grow.

....

LOUISE DRISCOLL

Friends give full color to our lives; they help us sharpen our

focus, giving a clearer picture of all the beautiful, simple

things that really matter.

Delicate threads of hope, patiently woven become the strong fabric of our faith.

In the presence of hope—faith is born. In the presence of faith, love becomes a possibility! In the presence of love— miracles happen!

May the God of hope fill you with all joy and peace as you trust in him.

....

ROMANS 15:13 NIV

Heaven's love is
spoken in the
language of your heart.

Kindness...is the
poetry of the heart, the
music of the world.

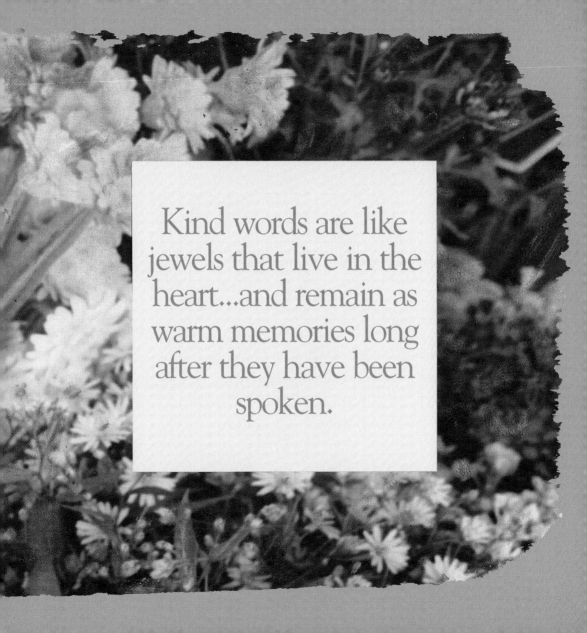

Kind words are like jewels that live in the heart...and remain as warm memories long after they have been spoken.

God's fingers can touch nothing but to mold it into

loveliness.

....

GEORGE MACDONALD

It is God...who made the garden grow in your hearts.

....

1 CORINTHIANS 3:6 TLB

He loves each one of us, as if there were only one of us.

....

AUGUSTINE

*God's touch…
lights the
world with
color and
renews our
hearts with
life.*

Tender hearts
need tender
care.

Blessed are the ones God sends to show His love
for us…our friends.

Love is the sweet, tender, melting nature of God
flowing from His heart.

May you wake each day with His blessings and
sleep each night in His keeping, and may you
always walk in His tender care.